POMPOMANIA
Christine Leech

quadrille

Photography by Joanna Henderson

Publishing Director Sarah Lavelle
Commissioning Editor Lisa Pendreigh
Editorial Assistant Harriet Butt
Creative Director Helen Lewis
Designer Gemma Hayden
Assistant Designer Vanessa Masci
Production Director Vincent Smith
Production Controller Tom Moore
Photographer Joanna Henderson
Stylist Christine Leech

First published in 2016 by
Quadrille Publishing Ltd
Pentagon House
52–54 Southwark Street
London SE1 1UN
www.quadrille.co.uk
www.quadrillecraft.com

Quadrille is an imprint of Hardie Grant
www.hardiegrant.com.au

Text, projects and designs
© 2016 Christine Leech
Photography
© Joanna Henderson
Artwork, design and layout
© Quadrille Publishing Ltd

British Library Cataloguing-In-
Publication Data
A catalogue record for this book
is available from the British Library.

ISBN 978 184949 674 2

10 9 8 7 6 5 4 3 2 1

Printed in China.

CONTENTS

INTRODUCTION

The most common refrain heard when I told people I was writing a book on pompoms was 'Oh, I used to make those as a child.' And so did I. I spent hours winding yarn onto basic cardboard pompom makers cut from cereal packets, then turning the results into fluffy chicks or monsters with big googly eyes. When I was asked to write this book, I was a little apprehensive about the time it can take to make a pompom and what exactly you might do with those simple spheres. I soon learnt that the humble cardboard maker has been replaced by more efficient plastic contraptions for speedy pompom making and that there are hundreds of things that you can do with your pompoms.

While some projects in this book are simple and require basic pompom-making techniques, others are more complex and involve a bit of brain power... but the results are amazing. Once you have got your head around the way a pattern is created within a pompom, there is no end to what you can create. The most exciting moment in pompom making comes when you cut through all the wraps of yarn and the pattern you hope you have created begins to reveal itself. There were many experiments when planning these projects, but even though some did not turn out just the way I expected, they all had a certain charm. Even the ones I initially considered a failure turned out pretty much okay after a hard trim with some sharp scissors. As in life, a good haircut can work wonders.

In this book I have used an acrylic DK-weight yarn from a company called Stylecraft (who were kind enough to give me many balls of yarn for experimentation). I recommend you also use a similar DK-weight yarn so that the number of wraps of each colour yarn are consistent with the instructions given. The colours mentioned in the instructions are specific to Stylecraft but it is easy to swap in colours based on whatever yarn you have to hand. When choosing yarns for your pompom making, inexpensive acrylic DK-weight yarns work best as they fluff up nicely when trimmed. Using an aran-weight or bulky yarn does mean less winding to fill the pompom maker, which makes for a speedier pom, but may give a less defined pattern. Some of the weirder and more wonderful yarns with sequins and fluffy bits make incredible pompoms, so do have fun and try lots of different types.

As I sit at my desk writing this introduction, I am surrounded by all the projects made for this book. I am struck by how versatile the humble pompom can be. When asked to write this book, never in my wildest dreams did I imagine I would be able to show you how to make pompoms in the shape of sushi!

Happy Pompoming!

BASIC POMPOM MAKING

Master these five steps and the pompom world is yours for the taking.

POMPOM MAKERS

Different types of makers are available that make the pompom process much easier.

FORK POMPOMS

You can buy tiny pompom makers, but they are fiddly to use and easy to lose. Forks are the perfect size to make smaller pompoms. Plus, if you are ever at a restaurant with a ball of yarn, well, there's your after-dinner entertainment right there.

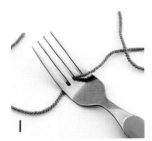

1

Cut a length of yarn to approximately 15cm (6 in). Place it between middle tines of a fork.

2

Wind yarn round fork 50 times, making sure cut end does not get caught up in wraps.

3

Once finished winding, use two cut ends to gather wraps tightly together. Tie into a knot.

4

If you find it tricky to pull yarn bundle tight, slip it off tines, gather and tie another knot.

5

Snip through each side of yarn bundle to release yarn strands.

6

Trim pompom with scissors into a neat, round shape. Keep brushing the strands to reveal any stray bits.

POMPOM PERFECTION

1 I find it easier to start wrapping yarn in the centre of a maker; it is less fiddly than trying to start at one end. With the fingers of one hand, hold the cut end of the yarn in place on the maker. Wind the yarn around the maker, catching the cut end under the wraps to hold it in place. If the instructions require you to wrap from one end, start in the centre then slide the yarn to the side once it is secure. Alternatively, tie the yarn on with a knot.

2 Wind the yarn evenly across the maker with a constant tension. It is easy to wind too much yarn in the centre of the maker halves and then the makers do not close properly. There is nothing worse than having your makers fly open after you have cut through all the wool and hundreds of strands of wool go falling to the floor. Believe me, I know!

3 Do not wrap the yarn round the maker too tightly as it is then harder to cut later. When you have complete a pompom use a good pair of sharp scissors, insert the tip of the blades between the two halves of the maker and snip.

4 After you have cut open your pompom, you need to tie another piece of yarn round the centre to stop all the bits falling out. Rather than tying a double knot straight away, tie one knot, wrap the yarn back on itself, pull tightly, then tie a double knot for a much tighter pompom.

5 Keep trimming. I learnt a lot making the pompoms for this book. My main realisation was that trimming is key! I went back to my basket of reject pompoms and realised that if I had spent more time with the scissors, carefully trimming round and round the pom I thought was a no-no, it would actually have been a yes-yes. Rolling the pompom between your hands moves the strands and shows up any bits that need a snip. Do this periodically as you trim for the perfect finish.

6 Cheat a little. There are some projects in this book that require lots of colour changes and small wraps of yarn. Once you have completed a project and trimmed the pompom, do not be afraid to pull out strands that make your pattern look uneven or even add ones in where there is a hole. Thread a large darning needle with the required colour and 'sew' it through the pompom in the necessary place, then trim. This method works well when adding eyes and highlights to faces, such as the inuit on pages 64–7.

7 Use the tip of a darning needle or the point of some scissors to move individual strands of yarn around. As pompoms are tied so tightly, when you move a strand it tends to stay in place. This is great for projects like the dia de muertos skull on pages 84–7, ensuring the colours for his eyes and teeth are in the right place.

TIP
Trim, trim and then trim some more.
The more you trim a pompom, the neater and
more obvious the pattern you have added inside
it becomes. Though as with hair, the wild,
tousled look sometimes works too!

LOOPED POMPOMS

Another fork method for making pompoms, but this time a sweet looped variety. Combining traditional fluffy pompoms with these loopy ones looks great on sweaters, socks, necklaces or cushions. There is not much that can't be improved by the addition of a pompom.

1
Cut a 15cm (6 in) length of yarn. Place it between middle tines of a fork.

2
Take ball of yarn and begin weaving strand from ball between tines, over and under each one.

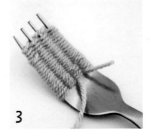

3
Work back and forth across tines until fork is completely full.

4
Using 15cm (6 in) length of yarn, gather woven yarn on tines together. Tie tightly into a knot.

5
To tighten knot gradually, slide woven yarn off of fork. Tighten as you go, then tie in a double knot.

6
Rearrange loops to neaten pompom and form a neat, round sphere.

Different types of yarn make different types of pompoms. Some make beautifully soft fluffy ones, which do not look like they are made from yarn at all. Other yarns do not work so well and you cannot get rid of the the knot in the middle. For the projects in this book, I found inexpensive acrylic yarn works best!

Glue gun tiny poms in different yarns to thin garden sticks. Ta-dah! A pretty year-round bouquet of flowers.

MULTIPLE POMPOMS

Sometimes you need a lot of pompoms... and you need them fast! For those emergency pompom moments, this method of making multiple poms is really handy.

1

Using an A5 notebook or a piece of card measuring approximately 21cm (8¼ in) in length, wrap yarn around card 70 times.

2

Slide the skein of yarn from the notebook or piece of card.

3

Starting 3cm (1¾ in) from end, tie a length of yarn around the skein in 6cm (2⅜ in) intervals, finishing 3cm (1¾ in) from end.

4

Using scissors, cut the skein into four. Cut through the loops of two pompoms at either end.

5

Shake the pompoms. Then trim. How much yarn you trim determines how neat your pompoms look (and how small they become).

TIP
If you want to make even more pompoms in one go, simply use a larger notebook or piece of card. You could also use a chair back or an obliging friend's pair of arms to wind the yarn round.

POMPOM LAMPSHADES

Use multiple pompoms to decorate old lampshades
that have seen better days. Remove the fabric
coverings and spray the frames with black paint.
Use a glue gun to stick different shapes and colours
of pompoms in place. For safety, remember to use
a low-emissions light bulb though.

NO-HASSLE TASSELS

A great partner to the pompom is the tassel. These are super-quick and can be made in any size and shade. I have made some small ones to give my Dala Horse a brightly coloured mane, but they are also great added to jewellery, bag charms, garlands and chandeliers.

1

Cut a rectangle of card to height you want finished tassel to be. Cut a length of yarn to approximately 15cm (6 in). Lay it alongside card.

2

Wrap yarn around card and over cut length of yarn. The more wraps, the plumper the tassel. These mini ones are made with 25 wraps of yarn.

3

When complete, use cut piece of yarn to tie a double knot tightly around yarn bundle. Slide yarn bundle off of piece of card.

4

Tie another cut length of yarn around yarn bundle, approximately one quarter of way down from tied end.

5

Cut bottom edge of bundle to release strands of yarn. Trim to neaten. Use yarn tails or a glue gun to fix tassel in place.

TIP

For multi-coloured tassels, wrap two or three yarns in different shades around the card at the same time. For tassels with a different coloured core, first wrap one colour then cover with another. For stripey tassels, wrap blocks of different colours next to each other.

ONE-COLOUR
POMPOMS

RAINCLOUD MOBILE

This pretty mobile is perfect for a nursery or child's room. Make the raindrops in coloured yarns to match the decorative scheme.

YOU WILL NEED

For the cloud:
DK-weight acrylic yarn in the following colours: silver, parma violet, sunshine

For the raindrops:
DK-weight acrylic yarn in the following colours: sherbert, royal, atlantis, white, midnight, bluebell, turquoise, cloud blue, emperor, aster

3.5cm (1⅜ in), 5.5cm (2⅛ in), 9cm (3½ in) and 11.5cm (4½ in) diameter pompom maker

Darning needle

Make pompoms in the following sizes and colours:
1 x 11.5cm (4½ in) in a mixture of silver and parma violet
1 x 9cm (3½ in) in parma violet
1 x 9cm (3½ in) in silver
1 x 5.5cm (2⅛ in) in silver
1 x 5.5cm (2⅛ in) in parma violet
1 x 3.5cm (1⅛ in) in silver
1 x 5.5cm (2⅛ in) in sunshine

1

Thread darning needle with yarn tails and use to attach smaller pompoms to largest. Sew until all poms are firmly joined.

2

Add smallest 3.5cm (1⅜ in) pompom underneath 11.5cm (4½ in) one. Then add two 9cm (3½ in) pompoms either side.

3

Fix two 5.5cm (2⅛ in) pompoms in between the 9cm (3½ in) ones to make a cloud shape.

4

Fix 5.5cm (2⅛ in) sun pompom to back of cloud, so sun appears to be just peeking over cloud.

CONTINUED...

TO MAKE THE RAINDROPS

Make three 5.5cm (2⅛ in) pompoms in atlantis, turquoise, and aster, then make 3.5cm (1⅜ in) pompoms from the rest of the colours. When cutting the yarn, make sure you leave long tails for tying the raindrop pompoms to the cloud.

1

Remove pompom from maker. Start trimming pompom into a cone shape.

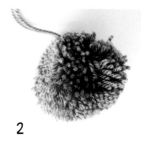

2

Cut into pompom at an angle towards yarn tails used to tie pom together.

3

Trim all around yarn tails to make a neat cone-shaped pompom.

4

Trim bottom of pompom into a neat round shape. Keep trimming until you are happy with the shape.

5

Trim away one yarn tail. Thread darning needle with remaining tail and attach it to base of cloud.

TIP
When trimming your pompoms, keep brushing the yarn between cuts to keep the shape neat.

POMSAI TREES

There is something very zen and calming about these pomsai trees. They make great deskmates and do not require quite as much maintenance as their living bonsai counterparts.

Make a selection of pompoms in different sizes and shades of green. For the larger tree, I made 1 x 7cm (2¾ in), 2 x 5.5cm (2⅛ in), 5 x 3.5cm (1⅜ in) pompoms, and 4 x small ones made on a fork (see page 9). For the smaller tree, I made 2 x 5.5cm (2⅛ in) pompoms, 5 x 3.5cm (1⅜ in) and 2 x small ones made on a fork. Trim them all so they are compact and spherical.

To fix the pompoms to the twig trunk:

1 Luckily I had these beautiful stones from a beach in Croatia, where many had natural holes, which makes them a perfect stand for the pomsai. If you can find similar pebbles, then brilliant. If not, a lump of air-dry modelling clay works too.

2 Trim your twig to about 12cm (4¾ in) high, then form the clay into a pebble shape and insert the twig. Make sure the pebble shape has a stable base to stand on and the twig remains upright.

3 As with real bonsai, try to visualize what the final tree will look like. Begin with the largest pompoms and glue gun one to the trunk. Working your way around the tree, keep adding further pompoms until it looks pleasing from all angles.

FOOTSTOOL

This footstool never fails to raise a smile from visitors to my house.
A great way of using up scraps of yarn, there is everything from chunky
aran to fluffy angora and cotton DK here. Choose a range of colours;
I went for neutral shades of grey, beige and white to allow the brighter
accents of pink, orange and turquoise to stand out.

YOU WILL NEED

Small footstool,
the body of this one
is approximately 10cm
(4 in) deep with
a diameter of 40cm
(15¾ in)

Piece of stretchy soft
fabric that doesn't fray
(an old woollen sweater
or piece of jersey
cotton) in a colour
similar to your yarn

Various yarns in your
chosen colour scheme

3.5cm (1⅜ in), 5.5cm
(2⅛ in), 7cm (2¾ in) and
9cm (3½ in) diameter
pompom makers

Scissors

Darning needle

2 metres ribbon

1 Make lots of pompoms in various sizes and colours. For this footstool, I made 100 pompoms! Most are one colour, but for some I wound two or three shades together for a multi-coloured effect. To do this, hold all the yarns together as you wind them onto the maker. Leave long yarn tails when tying the pompoms as these are used to sew them to the footstool.

2 Measure the padded part of your footstool, as shown below.

3 Depending on the shape of your stool, cut a circle or square from stretchy fabric using this measurement. Thread the darning needle with ribbon, then sew a running stitch all round the edge. Leave a long length of ribbon at the beginning and end.

4 Place the fabric over the stool pad and gather it on the underside by pulling the ribbon ends. Once it is fitting snugly, knot the ribbon.

5 To sew the pompoms to the fabric, thread the darning needle with the yarn tail of one pompom then stitch it securely in place anywhere on the cover. Repeat with the second tail. Tie the tails together and trim.

6 Repeat with the remaining pompoms until the fabric is covered. Vary sizes so the small pompoms fill the gaps between the large ones.

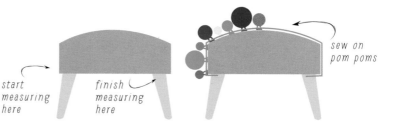

*start
measuring
here*

*finish
measuring
here*

*sew on
pom poms*

TIPS

You can use a glue gun to fix the pompoms to the footstool, but there is no going back once they're stuck.

If you don't have a footstool, this method also makes a really cute rug.

GIANT GARLAND

This garland uses one whole ball of yarn per pompom. Fortunately you do not need to wind the yarn onto a pompom maker... because that would take forever! You simply use the ball of yarn as is.

YOU WILL NEED

For the pompoms:
1 ball of aran-weight acrylic yarn in the following colours: spice, teal, bluebell, aspen, fondant

Scissors

2 metres (2 yards) gold ribbon, plus extra ribbons for decoration

TIP
This garland is shown above an unlit fireplace for display purposes only. Acrylic yarn and an open fire are never a good mix!

1
Wrap a 50cm (20 in) length of yarn around centre of ball. Tie tightly. Wrap and tie again, this time with a double knot.

2
Cut through loops of yarn on one side. There will be really small loops in centre of the ball, so make sure you snip all of them.

3
The ball of yarn now looks like a giant tassel. Cut through loops on other side. Shake ball to leave a messy mass of yarn.

4
Trim any long strands so ball looks pompom-like. Keep ties round centre separate. Use ties to fix pompoms to ribbon.

PAJAKI CHANDELIER

This pompom-adorned chandelier is based on a traditional
Polish decoration called a Pajaki, which are normally made
from coloured paper and straws.

YOU WILL NEED

*For the pompoms
and tassels:*
DK-weight acrylic yarn
in the following colours:
citron, sunshine,
twilight pearl, aspen,
meadow, sunshine,
green

3.5cm (1 3/8 in) and
5.5cm (2 1/8 in) diameter
pompom makers

Scissors

Fork

Gold embroidery
thread

Inside ring of a 25cm
(9 3/4 in) diameter
wooden embroidery
hoop

Washi tape

5 metres (5 yards)
gold cord

Darning needle

Glue gun

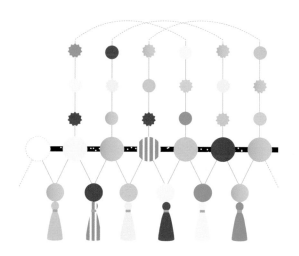

Using all the yarn colours, make 6 x 3.5cm (1 3/8 in) pompoms,
6 x 5.5cm (2 1/8 in) pompoms, 9 small fork pompoms (see page 9),
9 looped fork pompoms (see page 12), and 6 tassels (see page 17).
To make the tassels use a postcard-sized piece of card, measuring
15cm x 10cm (6 x 4 1/4 in). Wrap the yarn 20 times around the card
and then use gold embroidery thread to fasten the tassel.

These pompoms and tassels are threaded onto gold cord in the next
steps. The diagram above shows the different colours and the order
in which I placed them to create the chandelier shown opposite.

1 Cover the outside edge of the embroidery hoop with washi tape.

2 Cut three 70cm (27 1/2 in) lengths and six 40cm (15 3/4 in) lengths
of gold cord.

CONTINUED...

Thread darning needle with 70cm (27½ in) cord. Pass through three small and looped poms alternately.

Repeat with two more cord lengths, plus six more small and looped poms. Mix up the colours.

Thread darning needle with 40cm (15¾ in) cord. Pass through tassel, then through 3.5cm (1⅜ in) pom.

Using glue gun, fix 5.5cm (2⅛ in) poms to hoop, each spaced equally apart.

Tie one end of a 70cm (27½ in) cord behind one pom on hoop. Tie other end behind opposing pom.

Repeat with remaining cord lengths. Hang from a hook to work comfortably on next step.

Using glue gun, fix each 40cm (15¾ in) cord to hoop so tassel hangs between poms on hoop.

Separate cords so there is a 'V' shape between each pompom. Trim away any untidy ends.

MULTI-
COLOURED
POMPOMS

UNDERSTANDING POM-STRUCTION

Now you have mastered the simple, single-colour pompom, it is time to tackle multi-coloured poms. Multi-coloured pompoms can be as straightforward as making half in one shade and the other half in a different shade. More complex multi-coloured pompoms – where a design is added into the pompom itself by cleverly winding layers of colours in strategic positions – can include stripes, spots, hearts, flowers and even faces.

Before I explain how to make these trickier multi-coloured pompoms, I need to reiterate one thing. It's back to The Most Important Fact Ever When Making a Pompom: you need to wind yarn over both parts of the pompom maker. Too many times I have had to tell people that, because they have only used one of the hinged parts of their maker, they are never going to be able to complete their pompom. It has led to tears.

MEET YOUR MAKER

It is crucial to understand your pompom maker. Think of the maker as being divided into two halves, with one half being the front and the other the back.

For a pompom that is the same pattern all over (like the raspberry ripple ice cream scoop on page 71) or with an identical front and back (like the California roll sushi on page 58), then you wind the same pattern of yarns on both halves of the maker.

If you are making a pompom with a design on the front (like the heart on page 79), then you wind the pattern on one maker (the front) and fill the other maker (the back) with a single colour to complete the pompom.

If you are making a complex character pompom (like the birdie on pages 92–5) then the front maker is used to create the face and the back maker to create the back of his head.

back half

front half

ABBREVIATIONS

F	Front half of maker
B	Back half of maker
LHE	Left-hand edge
RHE	Right-hand edge

IT'S ALL ABOUT SYMMETRY

When I first experimented with pompom making, I was not sure I would ever make anything more complex than a two-colour stripey pompom. But as I worked out how a pompom is formed on the maker, I began to understand what happens when I wind coloured yarns in different ways. It's all about symmetry.

When completing a pompom, as you cut the yarn around the middle of the maker, the pompom divides at that cut and you have exactly the same pattern on the left-hand and right-hand sides. Once you have comprehended this, you can start making patterns and shapes inside the pompoms.

FIRST AND LAST

As a pompom is spherical, the first wrapping of yarn on the front half of the maker ends up being the centre front of the pompom (for example, the beak of the bird or the central line of the heart). The last wrapping will be the place where the front half joins the back half. Because of this fact, you often wind half as many wraps of yarn in these two places as they double in quantity when you remove the maker.

PUTTING PATTERN INTO A POMPOM

Before making a pompom, I first work out the design. Here are the steps I took when planning the birdie. He is nicely symmetrical, so a good example to use to explain the principles of designing a pompom.

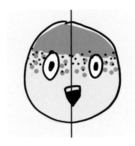

CHEAT A LITTLE

There are some projects in this book that require lots of colour changes and small wraps of yarn. When you have completed a project and trimmed the pompom, do not be afraid to pull out any coloured strands that make your pompom look uneven. Equally, you can add extra strands of yarn anywhere there is a gap.

1 First I made a sketch of what I wanted the design – in this case, the birdie – to look like.

2 Starting with his head, I found the line of symmetry running down through his beak. This is the centre front of the pompom. The first wraps of yarn will make his beak.

Thread a darning needle with the required colour yarn. Stitch it through the pompom in the exact spot, then trim. This method works well when adding eyes and highlights to faces (like the inuit on pages 64-7 and the emoji-poms on pages 80-3).

front half   back half

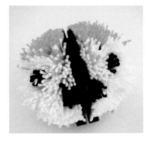

You can also use the point of a darning needle or the tip of some scissors to move individual strands around within the pompom. This works well for projects like the sushi on pages 56-9 and the dia de muertos skull on pages 84-7, making sure all the colours sit in the right place.

3 This is what the design looks like drawn as a template, showing the different colour wraps and layers of yarn.

4 If you follow the template or instructions, the actual pompom looks like this before it's removed from the maker.

WORKING THE WEDGE

A wedge is a very useful shape to master when it comes to making patterned pompoms, as it allows you to make shapes like spots, hearts, noses and mouths.

BUILDING A WEDGE

Instead of placing each winding of yarn adjacent to the previous wraps in a flat layer, a wedge is built up so the yarn is higher on one side or in the centre.

Begin by winding a base layer of yarn, working from left to right and then work back and forth across the maker. However, each time you reach the left-hand edge, work slightly fewer wraps. In doing this, you will have more wraps of yarn at the right-hand edge than the left.

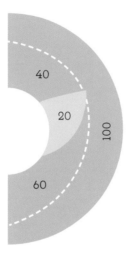

40

20

100

60

When shown on a template, a wedge looks like this...

After you have wound the 20 wraps of blue yarn to build up the wedge, then wind the second colour yarn across the rest of the maker, bringing the second yarn up to the same level as the wedge in the first yarn. The white dotted line indicates the level of this first layer of yarn wraps.

To make a spot or a circle (like the inuit's face on page 64–7), then make a wedge that is widest in the centre than it is at the two sides.

On the pompom maker, a wedge looks like this. One side is noticeably fuller than the other, with more wraps of yarn.

In the finished pompom, a wedge looks like this. It is easy to tease this shape into neat, straight lines while trimming.

GO-GO GARLAND

These bold pompoms make for a pretty garland. The addition of weighty wooden beads helps it to hang nicely. Wind the front and back halves of the maker with different shades of yarns to create multi-coloured pompoms.

YOU WILL NEED

For the pompoms:
DK-weight acrylic yarn in the following colours: shrimp, soft peach, stone, sherbert, metallic gold (I used Bergere de France Metalika in etoile)

5.5cm (2⅛ in) maker

Scissors

16 wooden beads, 20mm (³⁄₁₆ in) in diameter

1 metre (1 yard) leather thonging

TIP
Sparkly gold yarn is too thin for pompom making; it takes a lot of yarn and winding. Mix the gold with a similar coloured yarn for the same sparkly effect.

1 Make one pompom in each colour combination shown below. On a 5.5cm (2⅛ in) maker, wind approximately 220 wraps to fill each half.

2 Thread the pompoms onto the leather. Gently squeeze a pompom between your fingers and thumb around the centre. You should feel it 'gives' more in one place. Thread the leather through the pompom at this point (where a hole is left when the pompom is tied). Using a large darning needle and thicker yarn or ribbon to thread pompoms can pull out several strands. I find it easier to place the leather thonging end between the arms of a kirby grip and sellotape in place.

3 Thread the pompoms and wooden beads alternately onto the leather thonging until you have completed the garland. Thread two or three extra beads at each end and knot securely.

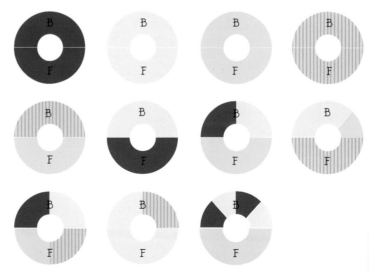

SPOTTY & STRIPEY POMS

Learning to make spots and stripes is the first step towards more complex patterns. Practising these will help you master other projects. They are also a good way to get to grips with templates.

YOU WILL NEED

For the pompoms:
DK-weight acrylic yarn in the following colours: apricot, denim, citron, white, aspen, fondant, lime, magenta

5.5cm (2⅛ in) and 7cm (2¾ in) diameter pompom maker

Scissors

TIP

To learn how to make the simplest single spot pompom, follow the instructions for the Liquorice Allsorts on page 48, then trim the finished pompom into a neat sphere. Once you have mastered the single spot, try making a multi-spot pompom following the template on page 44.

I

For spot with outer ring, wind 40 wraps of apricot in centre of front maker in a wedge with widest part in centre. Wind 10 wraps of denim either side of wedge.

2

Wind 20 wraps of denim over apricot wedge. Then wind 30 wraps of apricot either side of denim.

3

Wind 40 wraps of apricot evenly to fill front maker. For a spot and ring on both sides, repeat steps 1–3 on back maker. For a plain side, fill back maker with wraps of apricot.

4

Complete pompom and remove it from maker. Trim pompom into a neat sphere.

1

2

3

For basic single stripe, wind 100 wraps of fondant over a 5.5cm (2⅛ in) maker, leaving far edges empty.

Wind 10 wraps of lime to fill empty spaces at both edges of maker.

Wind 20 wraps of lime across maker. Repeat on other half. Complete and remove from maker.

1

2

3

For beach ball stripe, wind 80 wraps of magenta over a 7.5cm (2¾ in) maker, leaving far edges empty.

Wind 160 wraps of white, again, stopping just short of RHE and LHE.

Wind 20 wraps of saffron to fill spaces at edges, then 40 wraps over entire maker. Repeat on other half.

1

2

3

For crossed stripes, wind 40 wraps of saffron evenly over one half of a 5.5cm (2⅛ in) maker.

Wind 30 wraps of saffron in centre in a wedge, keeping wedge 5 wraps wide and an even height.

Wind 40 wraps of lime each side of wedge. Repeat on other half. Complete and remove from maker.

SPOTS TEMPLATES

Spots like these are the foundation for projects such as the Sushi on page 57, and the round Liquorice Allsort on page 48.

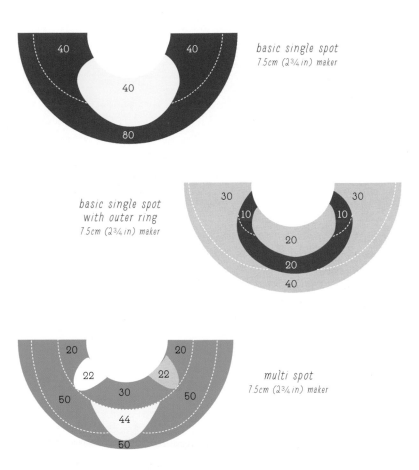

basic single spot
7.5cm (2¾in) maker

basic single spot
with outer ring
7.5cm (2¾in) maker

multi spot
7.5cm (2¾in) maker

STRIPES TEMPLATES

Stripes like these are the foundation for projects, such as the Macapom on page 47, the striped Liquorice Allsort on page 51 and the Cactus on page 55.

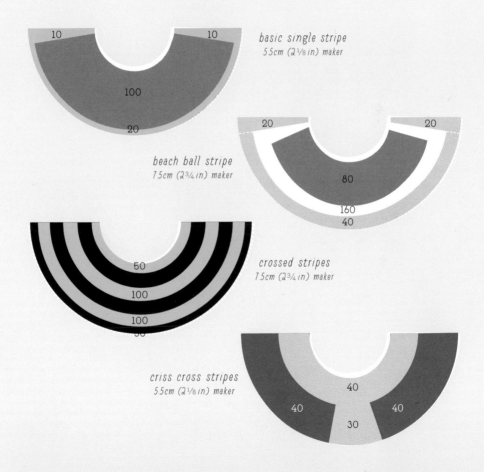

basic single stripe
5.5cm (2⅛in) maker

beach ball stripe
7.5cm (2¾in) maker

crossed stripes
7.5cm (2¾in) maker

criss cross stripes
5.5cm (2⅛in) maker

MACAPOMS

Take what is possibly the most photogenic of all French pâtisserie and mix it with the cutest craft discipline and what do you get? The macapom, of course.

YOU WILL NEED

DK-weight acrylic yarn in the following colours: white, aspen, emperor, bluebell, fondant, cream, bright pink, soft peach, walnut, mocha, camel

5.5cm (2⅛ in) diameter pompom maker

Scissors

1

Starting at LHE, wrap 'filling' colour 40 times around one half of maker.

2

Wrap 'shell' colour 140 times around maker. Repeat on other half. Complete pompom and trim it into a neat sphere.

TIP

For macaron shells with a speckled effect, simply wrap two colours (the main colour yarn and a yarn a couple of shades lighter or darker) across the centre of one half of the pompom maker as you are reaching the maker's capacity.

3

Flatten pompom between your palms. Holding it between your thumb and forefinger, trim the sides. Trim top and base shorter for a flatter shape.

4

Carefully trim 'filling' shorter than 'shell'. Continue trimming until you are happy with shape. Repeat with other colours for more macapoms.

LIQUORICE ALLSORTS

Liquorice Allsorts are in my Top Five Sweets Of All Time. The yellow or pink coconut rolls are my faves. Guess what?! You can buy packets of just those ones. They should be called Liquorice Sorts.

YOU WILL NEED

DK-weight acrylic yarn in the following colours: white, black, fondant, citron, walnut and aster

3.5cm (1⅜ in) and 5.5cm (2⅛ in) diameter pompom makers

Scissors

1 Wind 20 wraps of black at centre of one half of a 3.5cm (1⅜ in) maker, creating a wedge.

2 Wind 30 wraps of citron (or fondant) on both sides of black wedge.

TIP
To make the nasty blue one (the one that gets left in the packet until you are desperate for something to eat) wind three shades of blue yarn together across a 3.5cm (1⅜ in) maker.

3 Wind 30 wraps of citron evenly over entire maker. Fill other half of maker with citron. Complete and remove from maker.

4 With black spot top and bottom, trim pompom into a neat round, then trim top and base into a slightly flatter shape.

CONTINUED...

TO MAKE THE PRETTY STRIPEY ALLSORT

The most common of the Allsort family, this three-layer delicacy comes in various colourways but always with a centre liquorice stripe.

I	2	3
Wind 60 wraps of white on a 3.5cm (1⅜ in) maker, leaving far edges empty. Wind 30 wraps of black, filling gaps at edges.	Repeat on other half of maker using walnut (or fondant or aster) and black. Complete and remove from maker.	Flatten pompom with white and walnut top and bottom. Trim sides into a square. Trim top and base into a flatter shape.

TO MAKE THE SUPER-SIZE ALLSORT

You do not get many of these Allsorts per pack, but it is the sweetie that everyone wants as it is simply massive.

I	2	3
Wind 75 wraps of white on a 5.5cm (2⅛ in) maker, stopping before both edges. Wind 50 wraps of black, filling half of empty gaps at both edges.	Wind 30 wraps of pink over black, filling in rest of empty spaces on both sides. Repeat on other half of maker. Complete and remove from maker.	Flatten pompom with white top and bottom. Trim sides into a square. Trim top and base into a flatter shape.

CACTI

These cacti pompoms are a lot less prickly
than their living counterparts.

YOU WILL NEED

*DK-weight acrylic yarn
in the following colours:*
meadow, saffron, green,
lime

3.5cm (1³⁄₈ in). 5.5cm (2³⁄₈ in)
and 7.5cm (2¾ in) diameter
pompom makers

Scissors

Small plant pot

1

For mottled cactus, wind
15 wraps of meadow over
right half of front maker.
Wind 2 wraps of saffron
around centre of maker
and trim back yarn ends.

2

Wind wraps of meadow
over left half. Wind
meadow back and forth,
interspersed with 2 wraps
of saffron at random
intervals, to fill maker.

3

Repeat steps 1–2 on back
maker. Complete pompom
and remove it from maker.
Repeat all steps using
a 3.5cm (1³⁄₈ in) maker
to make three smaller
pompoms.

4

Roughly trim larger
pompom into an oval
with a flat base. Trim the
smaller pompoms with
flat bases. Using glue gun,
fix mini-poms to main
pompom body.

CONTINUED...

If you want your cactus
to flower, make some
tiny pink pompoms
using the fork method
(see page 7). Trim them
to a neat size and then
join them to the top
of your main cactus.

TO MAKE THE STRIPEY CACTUS

1

For stripey cactus, wind 40 wraps of green over front maker.

2

Wind 50 wraps of lime to cover evenly the previous green layer.

3

Continue in alternate layers as follows: 80 wraps green, 50 wraps lime, 80 wraps green, 50 wraps lime, 40 wraps green.

4

Repeat steps 1-3 on back maker. Complete pompom and remove it from maker. With stripes vertical, roughly trim into a flat base, keeping yarn strands long on rest of pompom.

5

Carefully separate the lime and the green stripes. Trim back some of green to make lime strands stand out like spines of a cactus.

6

Work around pompom, trimming back each green section. If preferred, add small pink flowers to cactus (see left). Place in a suitable small plant pot and display.

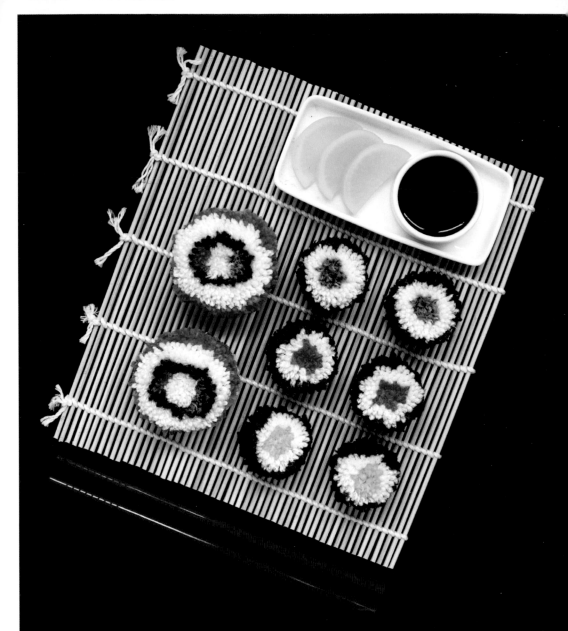

SUSHI

How cute is this pompom sushi? From a distance it's fairly hard
to tell it's not real... although it quickly becomes obvious
when you try and take a bite.

YOU WILL NEED

*DK-weight acrylic yarn
in the following colours:*
shrimp, white, cream,
green, greengage, jaffa,
peach, saffron

3.5cm (1⅜ in) and
5.5cm (2⅛ in) diameter
pompom maker

Scissors

For salmon maki rolls,
wind 10 wraps of shrimp
in centre of 3.5cm (1⅜ in)
front maker.

Wind 5 wraps of cream
and white together either
side of shrimp, then 5
wraps over shrimp.

To make egg maki rolls,
follow the instructions for
the salmon maki rolls but
use saffron for the centre
instead of shrimp. For
cucumber maki rolls, use
greengage for the centre.

Wind 35 wraps of green
over maker. Repeat
steps 1–3 on back maker.
Complete using strands
of shrimp to tie it together.
Remove from maker.

Holding pompom around
green centre, trim white and
shrimp side flat. Repeat on
opposite side. Trim green
into a cylindrical shape.

1

For California rolls, wind 10 wraps of greengage just off centre of a 5.5cm (2⅛ in) maker.

2

Wind 15 wraps of peach to left of greengage, then 5 wraps of shrimp to left of peach.

3

Wind 5 wraps of green either side of previous layer, then 10 wraps of green over previous layer.

4

Wind 10 wraps of white and cream each side of green, leaving far edges empty, then 45 across maker.

5

Wind a further 5 wraps of cream and white to cover any visible green.

6

Wind 40 wraps of shrimp and jaffa together over maker filling empty areas at edges of maker.

7

Repeat steps 1–6 on other half. Complete with strands of peach to tie pompom. Remove from maker.

8

Holding pompom around orange centre, trim cream, white and green side flat. Repeat on opposite side.

Trim orange centre into a cylindrical shape. Keep trimming until you are happy with the shape.

NICE PEAR

This pompom pear is unbelievably tactile. It looks best when trimmed hard, so do not be afraid to go at it with the scissors.

YOU WILL NEED

DK-weight acrylic yarn in the following colours: pomegranate, shrimp, meadow, lime, walnut

7cm (2¾ in) and 9cm (3½ in) diameter pompom makers

Scissors

Glue gun

1
For lower part, using a 9cm (3½ in) maker, wind 100 wraps of pomegranate in a wedge, leaving one quarter of maker empty at both RHE and LHE.

2
Wind 20 wraps of pomegranate and shrimp together over previous layer, covering wedge.

3
Wind 30 wraps of shrimp and meadow together over previous layer.

4
Wind 15 wraps of shrimp, meadow and lime together over previous layer.

CONTINUED...

5

Wind 20 wraps of meadow and lime to fill gaps at each edge, then 50 of meadow and lime to fill maker.

6

To finish, fill other half of maker with meadow and lime. Complete pompom and remove it from maker.

7

For top, using a 7cm (2¾ in) maker, wind 40 wraps of shrimp, meadow and lime across three quarters.

8

Fill maker with 120 wraps of meadow and lime. To finish, fill other half of maker with meadow and lime.

9

Complete pompom using three strands of walnut to tie it together. Remove it from maker.

10

Trim flat base of smaller and top and base of larger pompom. Fix together, matching speckled areas.

11

Trim the pompoms into a neat pear shape. Keep trimming until you are happy with the shape.

12

For the stalk, plait the three walnut strands together for 3–4cm (1¼ – 1½ in). Knot and trim.

INUIT & FIR TREE

A frosty wonderland of snow-covered fir trees and inuit fishermen makes for great Christmas decorations. For a more classic tree ornament, you could always replace the white yarn with green and add beads for baubles.

YOU WILL NEED

Yarn in the following:
khaki, white, walnut, bottle, lipstick, white, stone, parchment, aster, cream

3.5cm (1⅜ in), 5.5cm (2⅛ in) and 7cm (2¾ in) diameter pompom makers

Scissors

Glue gun

TIP
To make an igloo home for the inuit, make a 7.5cm (2¾ in) pompom using chunky white yarn. Trim the base flat. Make a 3.5cm (1⅜ in) pompom using white yarn but add a few wraps of black in the centre (see Liquorice Allsorts on page 48). Trim the base, front and back flat. Using a glue gun, join the pompoms.

1

For fir tree, wind 120 wraps of white across maker. Wind 40 wraps of white and khaki together, then 100 wraps of khaki to fill maker.

2

On other half of maker, wind 150 wraps of bottle, then 60 wraps of bottle and khaki together. Complete pompom and remove it from maker.

3

With tip at top, trim fir tree into a cone shape, trimming it short and neat at tip, but leaving strands longer at bottom for branches. Trim base flat.

4

For trunk, make a 3.5cm (1⅜ in) pompom using walnut. Trim bottom and top flat, then neatly round at sides. Using a glue gun, join tree to trunk.

TO MAKE THE INUIT

1

For body, using a 5.5cm (2⅛ in) maker, wind 15 wraps of cream and parchment, then adjacent 6 wraps of lipstick.

2

Starting slightly in from RHE, wind 40 wraps of lipstick. Wind 10 wraps of cream and parchment to fill gap at LHE.

3

Wind 15 wraps of white and aster together over lipstitck of previous layer, finishing 3 wraps from edge of lipstick at LHE.

4

Wind 80 wraps of white back and forth from RHE, finishing at edge of visible lipstick wraps. Wind 15 wraps of lipstick, then 8 wraps of cream and parchment at LHE until level.

5

To finish, starting at LHE, wind 25 wraps of cream and parchment, 40 wraps of lipstick, then 150 wraps of white on other half of maker. Complete pompom and remove it from maker.

6

Trim pompom into an oval, leaving lipstick strands slightly longer. Leave cream and parchment area down front of coat untrimmed. Trim top slightly flat. Trim base flat.

7

8

Inuit face (3.5cm/1³/₈ in maker)

Inuit body back (5.5cm/2¹/₈ in maker)

9

10

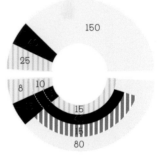

Inuit body front (5.5cm/2¹/₈ in maker)

Fir tree base (5.5cm/2¹/₈ in maker)

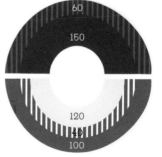

Fir tree top (5.5cm/2¹/₈ in maker)

For head, using a 3.5cm (1³/₈ in) maker, wind 20 wraps of stone in a wedge at centre of front maker, leaving one quarter empty at edges.

Wind 20 wraps of cream and parchment over maker, filling gaps. Wind 40 wraps of white over previous layer.

To finish, fill back maker with white. Complete and remove it from maker. Trim back of head into a neat round. Trim the face area flat. Leave long strands around face for fur hood.

Thread needle with black. Pull one strand through face to create eye. Trim flat. Repeat for second eye. Repeat with lipstick for a mouth. Using glue gun, join head and body.

ICE CREAM CONES

They may not taste as good as the real thing, but there's no chance
of these little beauties melting in the sunshine.

1

Wind 140 wraps of cream
and biscuit together over
a 7cm (2 ¾ in) maker
to make a two-tone
pompom, oval in shape.

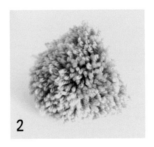

2

Roughly trim pompom at
one narrow end to make
a flat surface.

3

Neatly trim rest of
pompom into a pointed
cone shape.

4

Trim a slight indent in
top of flat surface for ice
cream scoop to sit inside.

YOU WILL NEED

*DK-weight acrylic yarn
in the following colours:*
red, cream, white,
fondant, aspen, aster,
citron, bright pink,
cream, biscuit

7cm (2¾ in) diameter
pompom maker

Scissors

Glue gun

TIP
Add choc chips to a scoop
by winding scattered
blocks of brown yarn into
a mint green pompom by
following the instructions
for the cactus on page 52.

CONTINUED...

LOVE HEARTS

A love heart pompom is the perfect gift for a loved one. When making the 'heart inside' pompom, keep picturing the shape of a heart as you wind the yarn and you will find it easier to build up the heart shape within the pompom.

YOU WILL NEED

DK-weight acrylic yarn in the following colours: light blue, dark blue, red

7cm (2¾ in) diameter pompom maker

Scissors

TIP
When trimming, to make a neater heart shape, keep brushing the yarn in different directions and trim where necessary.

TO MAKE THE HEART-SHAPED POMPOM

1

Make a pompom in the usual way. Complete and remove from maker, but do not trim it into a round.

2

Holding yarn tails in one hand, trim pompom into a conical shape to make bottom point of heart.

3

Cut a V-shaped groove in centre of upper half to make the top of heart.

4

Trim each side into a heart shape. Start at side then work round from front to back, trimming little bits.

CONTINUED...

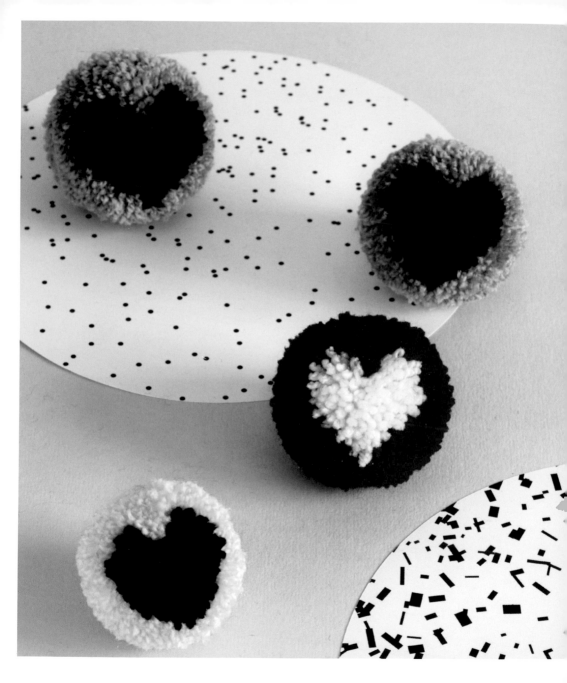

TO MAKE THE HEART-INSIDE POMPOM

1

For V shape, wind 12 wraps of blue, working one third in towards LHE. Make sure each strand lies flat and does not overlap.

2

Wind 8 wraps to right, then wind 6 wraps to left to build a wedge with widest part at LHE. Repeat this four times.

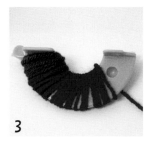

3

Wind 20 wraps of red, overlapping first 4 wraps of blue and working towards RHE, finishing one quarter in from RHE.

4

Wind 10 wraps of red back to left, starting 2 wraps in from previous layer. Then wind 50 wraps back and forth decreasing width of area to build a wedge with widest part at top.

5

Wind 60 wraps of blue back and forth starting in centre and working to RHE, filling right side of maker evenly. Wind 100 wraps of blue to fill entire maker. To finish, fill other half of maker with blue.

6

Complete and remove from maker. Trim pompom into a neat round. Keep trimming until you are happy with the shape. The harder you trim, the clearer the heart shape becomes.

EMOJI POMPOMS

This friendly crew of smiley pompoms are all made in a similar way.
Once you get the hang of how faces are created in pompom world,
you can make a whole set of emojis... maybe even the smiley poop.

YOU WILL NEED

*DK-weight acrylic yarn
in the following colours:*
black, citron, fondant,
turquoise

7cm (2¾ in) diameter
pompom maker

Scissors

TO MAKE THE SMILEY FACE EMOJI

For smile, one third in
from RHE, wind 5 wraps
of black and citron next
to each other. This keeps
smile straight when
cutting open pompom.

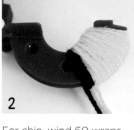

For chin, wind 60 wraps
of citron back and forth
from RHE, stopping at
black. If citron ends higher,
wind a couple more wraps
of black until level.

Wind 60 wraps of citron
back and forth from LHE,
stopping at black, filling
in empty part of maker.

For eyes, wind 8 wraps
of black over citron to
left of mouth.

CONTINUED...

EMOJI TEMPLATES

SMILEY EMOJI
Follow this diagram for the front half of the Smiley Emoji. For the back half, wind wraps of yellow yarn over the maker until full. Complete the pompom and remove from the maker.

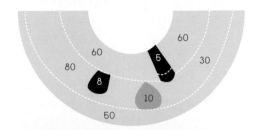

GRINNING EMOJI
Follow this diagram for the front half of the Grinning Emoji. For the back half, wind wraps of yellow yarn over the maker until full. Complete the pompom and remove from the maker.

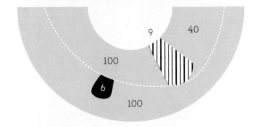

SURPRISED EMOJI
Follow this diagram for the front half of the Surprised Emoji. For the back half, fill the maker with yellow yarn. Thread a darning needle with white and sew highlights into the pupils.

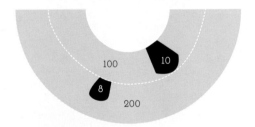

FEARFUL EMOJI
Follow this diagram for the front half of the Fearful Emoji. For the back half, from RHE to LHE, wind: 100 yellow, 40 yellow and blue, 80 blue. Match colour changes on front and back.

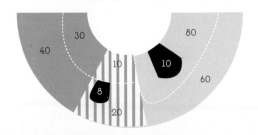

Wind 80 wraps of citron over left half of maker, including eyes.

Wind 30 wraps of citron over right half of maker, including mouth and chin.

Wind 10 wraps of pink in centre of maker. Then wind 50 wraps of citron to fill maker evenly.

To finish, fill back maker with citron. Complete and remove from maker.

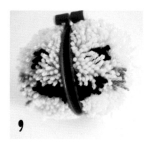

Trim the smiley face into a neat round. Keep trimming until you are happy with the shape. These emoji faces look best when neat and tidy.

TIP

By moving around individual strands of coloured yarn, you can really affect the expression of these little characters. Use either a needle or tiny scissors to position the strands of yarn, then trim.

DIA DE MUERTOS SKULL

A perfect pompom to make for a Hallowe'en celebration.
Although he's not remotely scary.

YOU WILL NEED

*DK-weight acrylic yarn
in the following colours:*
white, black, turquoise,
red, yellow, metallic
gold, bright pink

9cm (3⅛ in) diameter
pompom maker

Scissors

1
For nose, wind 10 wraps
of black in a wedge from
centre towards RHE. Wind
10 wraps of white next to
black. For teeth, wind 10
wraps of black and white
parallel, 2 wraps wide.

2
For chin, at RHE of
maker, wind 20 wraps of
turquoise and red together
in a wedge with widest
part at edge of maker.

3
Wind 20 wraps of white
between chin and teeth.
Wind 30 wraps of white
to left of nose. Wind 10
wraps of yellow over white
towards LHE. Wind 10
wraps of white until even.

4
For eye sockets, wind
60 wraps of gold, starting
a couple of wraps down
from top of yellow,
finishing a couple of
wraps up from nose.

CONTINUED...

5

Wind 15 wraps of turquoise over gold, starting and finishing a couple of wraps in from edges of gold. Then wind 10 wraps of black in centre of turquoise.

6

Wind 15 wraps of turquoise over black, then wind 60 wraps of gold over turquoise.

7

To complete eye socket, wind 10 wraps of yellow over gold. At LHE of maker wind 12 wraps of bright pink and red leaving a gap to yellow. Fill gap with 10 wraps of white.

8

Fill maker with white. There is already more yarn at LHE of maker due to the eye sockets; this helps to give a natural skull shape.

9

To complete pompom, fill other half of maker with white. Complete and remove it from maker.

10

Trim the skull so it is naturally pointy towards chin, but bulbous at crown. Keep trimming until you are happy with the shape.

POMPOMERANIAN

If someone is going to breed a dog so small and cute that it can fit in a teacup – and name it a Pomeranian – it would simply be rude not to recreate one made from pompoms.

YOU WILL NEED

DK-weight acrylic yarn in the following colours:
white, peach, pink, walnut, black, stone, parchment, cream

7.5cm (2¾ in) and 9cm (3½ in) diameter pompom makers

Scissors

Glue gun

TIP
Plait together several strands of contrast colour yarn to make a collar for your pompomeranian.

1 For nose, from centre towards RHE, wind 10 wraps of walnut in a wedge with widest part at centre. For tongue, wind 6 wraps of peach and fondant together to right of walnut.

2 For muzzle, wind 50 wraps of white and cream over right half in a wedge with widest part at centre. Stop before RHE. Wind 60 wraps of parchment over left half. Stop before LHE.

3 For eyes, wind 20 wraps of black at centre where cream and parchment meet, winding towards LHE for 4 wraps and then back and forth.

4 Wind 30 wraps of parchment to cover black eyes. Wind 90 wraps of parchment in a wedge over parchment and half of cream muzzle.

CONTINUED...

5

Wind 60 wraps of stone evenly over empty space at RHE and cream muzzle, stopping at parchment.

6

Wind 140 wraps of stone over maker, including space at LHE. Fill other half with stone. Complete pompom.

7

Trim face until features become clear. Leave yarn for muzzle and nose longer than eyes and forehead.

8

Trim back of head, leaving yarn longer for ears. Keep trimming until you are happy with the shape.

9

Add highlight to eyes by sewing a length of white yarn through each pupil, then trim.

10

For body, wind 110 wraps of cream and white from LHE to RHE of maker.

11

Wind 70 wraps of stone over cream and white. Fill other half with stone. Complete pompom.

12

Trim body base flat and chest slightly shorter than haunches and back. Using a glue gun, fix head to body.

HEY, BIRDIE

A fluffy little baby birdie who just wants someone to love him.

YOU WILL NEED

*DK-weight acrylic yarn
in the following colours:*
lemon, saffron, aspen,
white, walnut, black,
aster, turquoise

7cm (2¾ in) and 9cm
(3½ in) diameter
pompom maker

Scissors

Glue gun

1

For tummy, starting at
LHE, wind 16 wraps of
lemon towards centre.
Wind 8 wraps of lemon
and saffron together at
centre. Wind 16 wraps of
saffron, finishing at RHE.

2

Working back towards
LHE, wind 14 wraps of
saffron, 8 wraps of lemon
and saffron together,
then 11 wraps of lemon,
finishing just short of LHE.

TIP
Only got grey, black and
white yarn in your stash?
Don't worry. Those
shades make the most
perfect baby penguin.

3

Working towards RHE,
wind 11 wraps of lemon,
10 wraps of lemon and
saffron, then 60 wraps
of saffron in a wedge
with widest part at RHE.

4

Wind a further 7 wraps
of lemon and saffron
together and 8 wraps of
lemon, finishing at LHE.
Side on, there is more
yarn at bottom than top.

CONTINUED...

5

From LHE, wind: 40 aspen, 50 aster, 30 turquoise. On other half, wind: 80 aspen, 80 aster, 70 turquoise.

6

For beak, starting just off centre, wind 20 wraps of walnut in a wedge with widest part towards LHE.

7

Wind 80 wraps of lemon from RHE to beyond beak. Wind 10 wraps of lemon and aspen, then 50 aspen.

8

Wind 40 wraps of white from beak to third in LHE. Wind 10 wraps of black in centre, 3 wraps wide.

9

Wind 40 wraps of white over previous white layer. Wind 90 wraps of lemon over right half of maker.

10

Wind 10 wraps of lemon and aspen over remaining visible white. Wind 60 wraps of aspen at LHE.

11

On other half, wind: 230 aster and aspen. From RHE, wind: 40 lemon, 10 aspen and lemon, 15 aspen.

12

Complete pompoms. Trim body base and top flat, so head nestles in place. Trim breast shorter than wings.

13

Trim face, leaving beak and back. Trim head base flat. Trim beak into point. Using glue gun, fix head to body.

THANK YOU...

Firstly, a huge thank you to both Stylecraft and LoveKnitting
for providing balls and balls and balls of yarn.

Thank you to all at Quadrille, especially to Lisa and Harriet for having
the idea for this book in the first place and to Gemma for making
the book look great.

To the wonderful Jo for her fantastic photography and for going
above and beyond the call of pompom duty allowing us to use her
home as a location and her ironing board as a desk!

To everyone who I have taught how to make a pompom over the past year
or so – it was great to see so many people revisiting their childhood memories
and gasping in wonder at the advancements in pompom technology!

To Miss Violet Holloway for sharing with me her pompom skills
and her supercute pom-pup who inspired my own pompomeranian
– I hope you take some inspiration from this book.

To all the usual suspects... Mum, Dad, Jo, Ian, Oliver and Elliot (both
super-skilled pompom makers whose poms have made the cover of this
book), Jake, Kirsty and Laura, Lottie, Hannah – for letting us move every
single piece of furniture in her living room to get the shots just
right – and Stu (a prouder pompom producer I have yet to meet).

Here's to World Pomination!

stylecraftyarns.co.uk: Purveyors of the best yarn for making pompoms.

loveknitting.com: This website has everything you need to
get pompoming, from yarn galore to haberdashery bits 'n' bobs
and a variety of pompom makers.

hobbycraft.co.uk: Basically your go-to store for all things crafty.

tigerstores.co.uk: Tiger have a great set of pompom
makers in a variety of sizes.